FUN FACT FILE: FOUNDING FATHERS
20 FUN FACTS ABOUT
THOMAS JEFFERSON
By Jill Keppeler
Gareth Stevens
PUBLISHING
I0821907

Please visit our website, www.garethstevens.com. For a free color catalog of all our high-quality books, call toll free 1-800-542-2595 or fax 1-877-542-2596.

Library of Congress Cataloging-in-Publication Data
Names: Keppeler, Jill, author.
Title: 20 fun facts about Thomas Jefferson / Jill Keppeler.
Description: New York : Gareth Stevens, [2018] | Series: Fun fact file: Founding fathers | Includes index.
Identifiers: LCCN 2017004942| ISBN 9781538203149 (pbk. book) | ISBN 9781538202746 (6 pack) | ISBN 9781538202869 (library bound book)
Subjects: LCSH: Jefferson, Thomas, 1743-1826–Juvenile literature. | Presidents–United States–Biography–Juvenile literature.
Classification: LCC E332.79 .K46 2018 | DDC 973.4/6092 [B] –dc23
LC record available at https://lccn.loc.gov/2017004942

First Edition

Published in 2018 by
Gareth Stevens Publishing
111 East 14th Street, Suite 349
New York, NY 10003

Designer: Sam DeMartin
Editor: Ryan Nagelhout

Photo credits: Cover, p. 1 (background) MPI/Archive Photos/Getty Images; cover, p. 1 (portrait) Fine Art/Corbis Historical/Getty Images; p. 5 Roman Tirapolsky/Shutterstock.com; p. 6 Montesbradley/Wikimedia Commons; p. 7 Stokkete/Shutterstock.com; p. 8 N8Allen/Shutterstock.com; p. 9 MarmadukePercy/Wikimedia Commons; p. 10 Kean Collection/Archive Photos/Getty Images; p. 11 Valerii Iavtushenko/Shutterstock.com; p. 12 courtesy of the Library of Congress; p. 13 Victorian Traditions/Shutterstock.com; pp. 14, 16, 19, 20 (both) Everett Historical/Shutterstock.com; p. 15 GraphicaArtis/Archive Photos/Getty Images; p. 17 meunierd/Shutterstock.com; p. 18 Everett - Art/Shutterstock.com; p. 21 kateukraine/Shutterstock.com; p. 22 Morphart Creation/Shutterstock.com; p. 23 Robert Alexander/Archive Photos/Getty Images; p. 24 Alex Wong/Getty Images News/Getty Images; p. 25 Sean Pavone/Shutterstock.com; p. 26 Daniel M. Silva/Shutterstock.com; p. 29 Cvandyke/Shutterstock.com.

Printed in the United States of America

CPSIA compliance information: Batch #CS17GS: For further information contact Gareth Stevens, New York, New York at 1-800-542-2595.

Contents

Words in the glossary appear in **bold** type the first time they are used in the text.

The Third President

Thomas Jefferson is probably best known for writing the Declaration of Independence and serving as the third president of the United States. But there's a lot more that's interesting about this Founding Father!

Jefferson had many interests and hobbies. He liked to read, write, and learn about different things. These interests affected what Jefferson did as a leader of the country. Let's learn more about Thomas Jefferson and how he helped make the United States the country it is today!

Thomas Jefferson's face is on the $2 bill, but not many of these bills are made today. Jefferson is also on the nickel!

Young Thomas

FACT 1

Thomas Jefferson came from a big family. He had nine brothers and sisters!

Young Thomas was the third-oldest child and the oldest son in his family. Eight of the 10 children lived to be adults. As the oldest son, he **inherited** the family home when his father died. He was only 14 when that happened.

Thomas Jefferson was born April 13, 1743, in Shadwell, Virginia. The family home was destroyed in a fire in 1770. This marker stands at the site.

Jefferson said that, as a child, he practiced the violin 3 hours every day.

Jefferson took a small violin with him wherever he went!

Jefferson loved music and learned to play the violin, a stringed musical instrument, when he was a child. As an adult, he played the violin for Martha Wayles Skelton, the woman who later became his wife.

Builder and Inventor

FACT 3

Thomas Jefferson planned his home, Monticello, himself.

Jefferson was an **architect** who loved to design, or plan, buildings. Starting in 1768, he began working on his home, Monticello. The name is Italian for "little mountain." The home was mostly finished by 1784, but Jefferson later decided to tear parts down and rebuild them. It was finally done in 1809.

Today, many people still visit Monticello, which is located in Charlottesville, Virginia. The house is now a popular **museum**.

Jefferson invented a number of things—including a macaroni machine!

Jefferson liked **gadgets** and designed many of them. People who visit Monticello can still see some of Jefferson's creations. Among them is a book stand that could hold five books at once.

Jefferson liked macaroni, a kind of food he first tasted in Italy. He made this drawing of a macaroni machine about 1787.

FACT 5

Thomas Jefferson was one of the youngest men at the Second Continental Congress.

People often picture Jefferson as an old man, but he was only 32 when he first served as a **delegate** to the Second Continental Congress. This was a group of men who gathered to **represent** the 13 British North American colonies in 1775. Fighting in the American Revolution had started earlier that year.

This is what an artist imagined the Second Continental Congress looked like.

The Second Continental Congress first met at Independence Hall in Philadelphia, Pennsylvania.

FACT 6

Jefferson was not a great speaker.

Some US presidents are known for their speaking skills. But John Adams said of Jefferson: "During the whole time I sat with him in Congress, I never heard him **utter** three sentences together."

Making a Declaration

FACT 7

Thomas Jefferson wrote the Declaration of Independence in less than 3 weeks.

In 1776, the Continental Congress picked Jefferson and four other men (including John Adams and Benjamin Franklin) to write down why the colonies wanted to be free from Great Britain. Those men chose Jefferson to write the first **draft**. Jefferson got up every morning before the sun rose and wrote, tearing up many early copies. He finished in about 17 days.

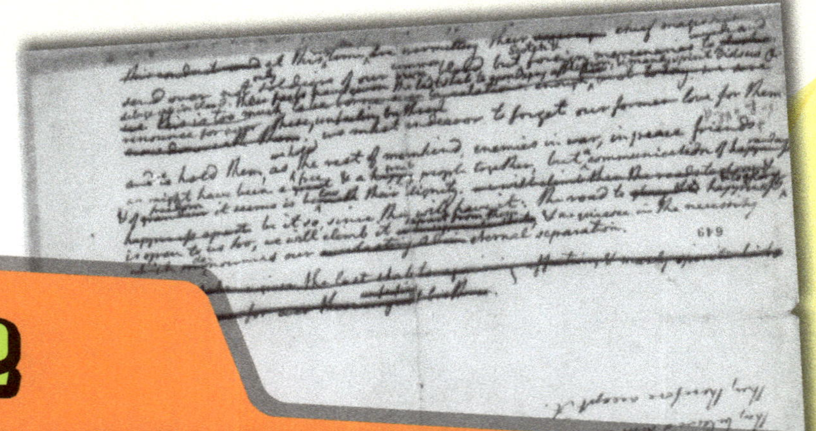

Jefferson crossed out sentences and changed his mind about words just like other writers do. This is part of one of his early drafts of the Declaration of Independence.

FACT 8

Thomas Jefferson gave Ben Franklin and John Adams a sneak peek.

After Jefferson finished his draft of the Declaration of Independence, he showed it to Franklin and Adams before giving it to the full group. The two men made some small changes.

This picture shows Benjamin Franklin, John Adams, and Jefferson looking at a draft of the Declaration of Independence.

Jefferson Gets Edited

FACT 9

The congress cut about a fourth of Thomas Jefferson's Declaration of Independence.

Jefferson and the others gave the rest of the congress this draft of the declaration on June 28, 1776. On July 2 through 4, 1776, the other members of the congress cut many of Jefferson's words, including a part against slavery.

Jefferson owned slaves himself, but wrote words attacking slavery in the Declaration of Independence.

FACT 10

Ben Franklin tried to cheer Jefferson up about the changes.

Jefferson later said that Franklin told him about a man whose store sign said: "John Thompson, Hatter, makes and sells hats for ready money." After people were done changing it, Franklin said, the sign just had a picture of a hat and the man's name.

Benjamin Franklin probably understood about editing. He was a famous writer and printer himself!

FACT 11

Thomas Jefferson escaped from British soldiers during the Revolution.

Jefferson did not serve as a soldier during the American Revolution. He returned home to Virginia, where he was elected governor in 1779. In 1781, a British general sent soldiers to capture Jefferson at Monticello, but the governor was warned and escaped.

One of the most famous battles of the revolution took place in Virginia. The Battle of Yorktown in September 1781 was the last major battle of the war.

FACT 12

Jefferson's daughters got to travel with him to France.

After the revolution, in 1784, the Continental Congress named Jefferson a **minister** to France. Jefferson's wife, Martha, had died in 1782. Jefferson took his daughters, Martha, 12, and Mary, 7, with him to France. There, they studied cooking and art.

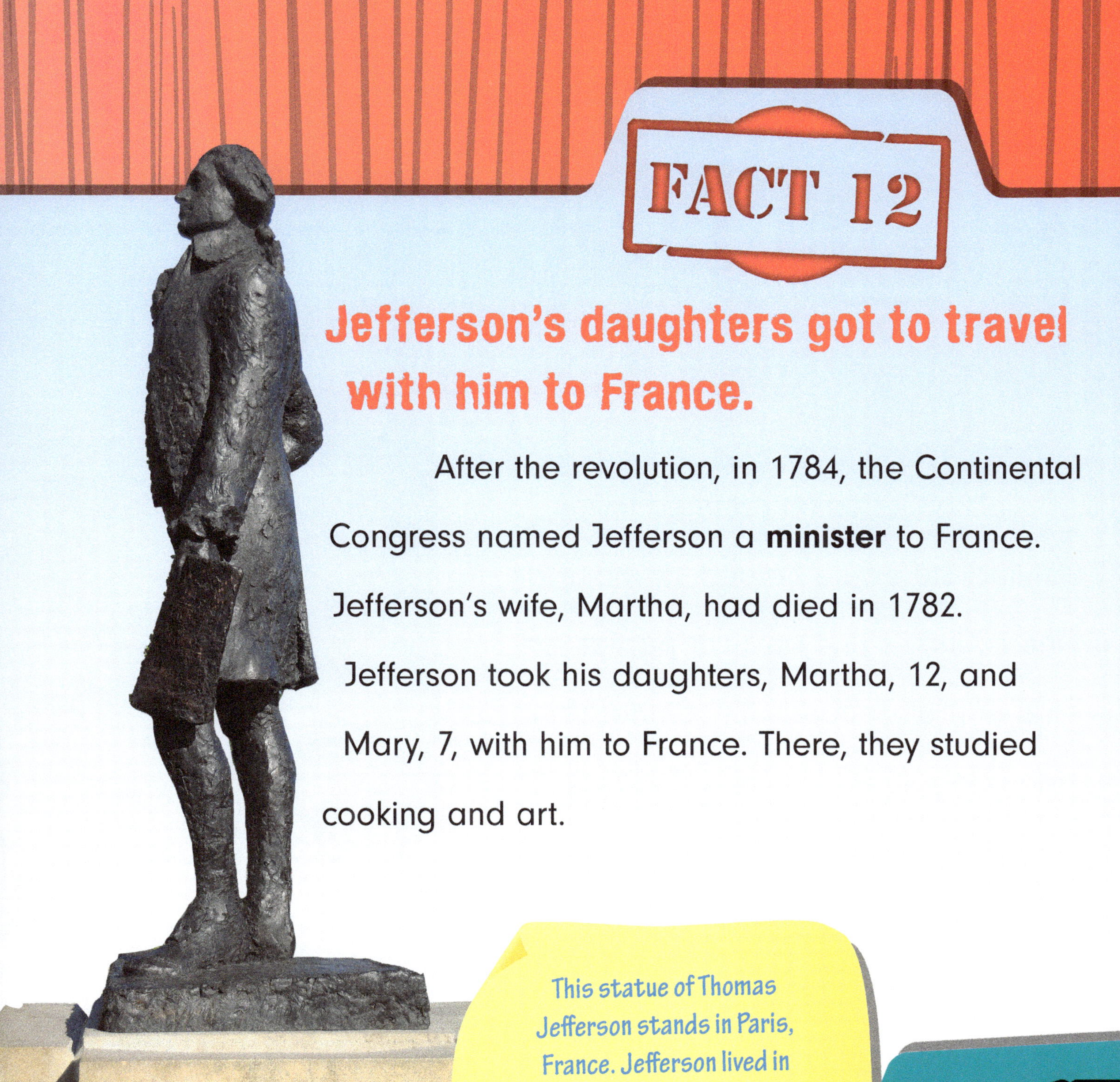

This statue of Thomas Jefferson stands in Paris, France. Jefferson lived in Paris from 1784 to 1789.

FACT 13

Thomas Jefferson helped found the Republican Party—sort of.

After Jefferson returned to the United States, he helped start one of the country's first political parties, or a group of people with comparable ideas about government. This was the Republican Party. However, it became the Democratic-Republican Party. Today, it's called the Democratic Party.

Jefferson returned from France in 1789. George Washington, the first president of the United States, made him the first secretary of state. This is one of the president's main advisors.

FACT 14

Jefferson and Aaron Burr tied for the office of president in the 1800 election.

In 1800, Jefferson ran for the presidency of the United States. When the votes were counted, Jefferson and Burr had the same number! Members of the US House of Representatives had to decide. They picked Jefferson.

Jefferson ran for president in 1796 as well, but he lost and became vice president instead. He was also elected president in 1804.

A Big Buy

FACT 15

Thomas Jefferson wasn't sure he was allowed to make the Louisiana Purchase—but he did it anyway.

Lewis

Clark

In 1803, Jefferson sent ministers to France to ask about buying a small amount of land in North America. France, however, offered to sell the United States a huge amount of land, which we now call the Louisiana Purchase. Jefferson took the deal.

Jefferson sent a group of explorers led by Meriwether Lewis and William Clark to explore the Louisiana Purchase. They left in 1803 and returned in 1806.

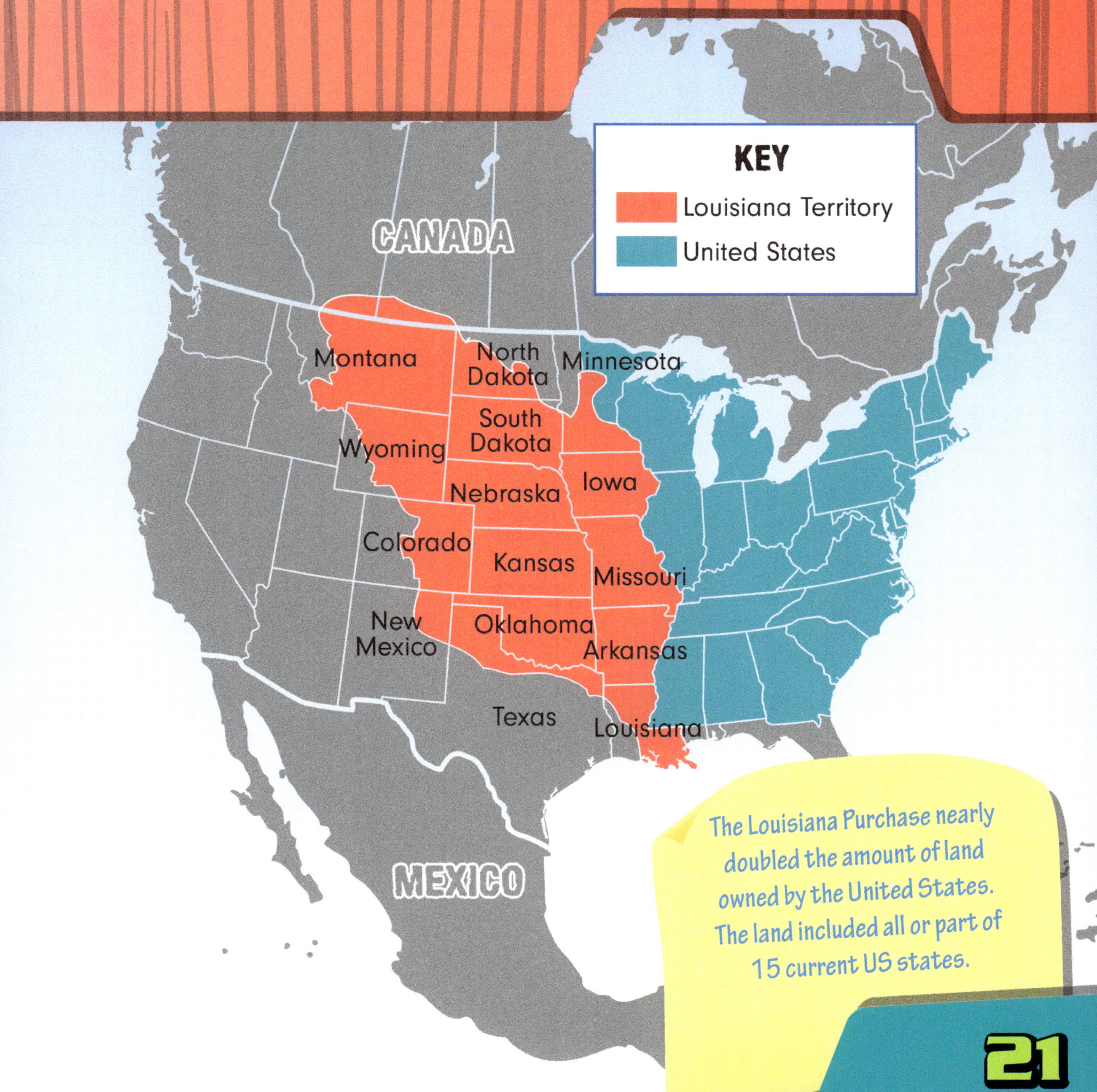

The Louisiana Purchase nearly doubled the amount of land owned by the United States. The land included all or part of 15 current US states.

A Mastodon in the House

FACT 16

Thomas Jefferson tried to build a mastodon skeleton in the president's house.

Jefferson was very interested in mastodons, ancient creatures much like elephants. While he was president, he had people send him mastodon bones. He tried to put together a mastodon skeleton in what is now the East Room of the White House!

Jefferson asked Lewis and Clark to watch for live mastodons (which he called "mammoths") when they explored the Louisiana Purchase.

Some of Jefferson's gardens have been re-created at Monticello. People can visit them today.

FACT 17

Jefferson really liked to grow things.

Jefferson liked other kinds of science, too, including **agriculture**. He kept careful track of his garden, including what worked and what didn't when growing crops. He grew many different kinds of fruits and vegetables and kept many notes.

A Love of Words

FACT 18

Thomas Jefferson wrote about 20,000 letters over his lifetime.

Jefferson wrote many letters to people and received many in return. Among the many people he **corresponded** with were John Adams, the second president of the United States, and Abigail Adams, John Adams's wife.

Jefferson used a machine called a polygraph to make copies of his letters. This is a copy of that machine.

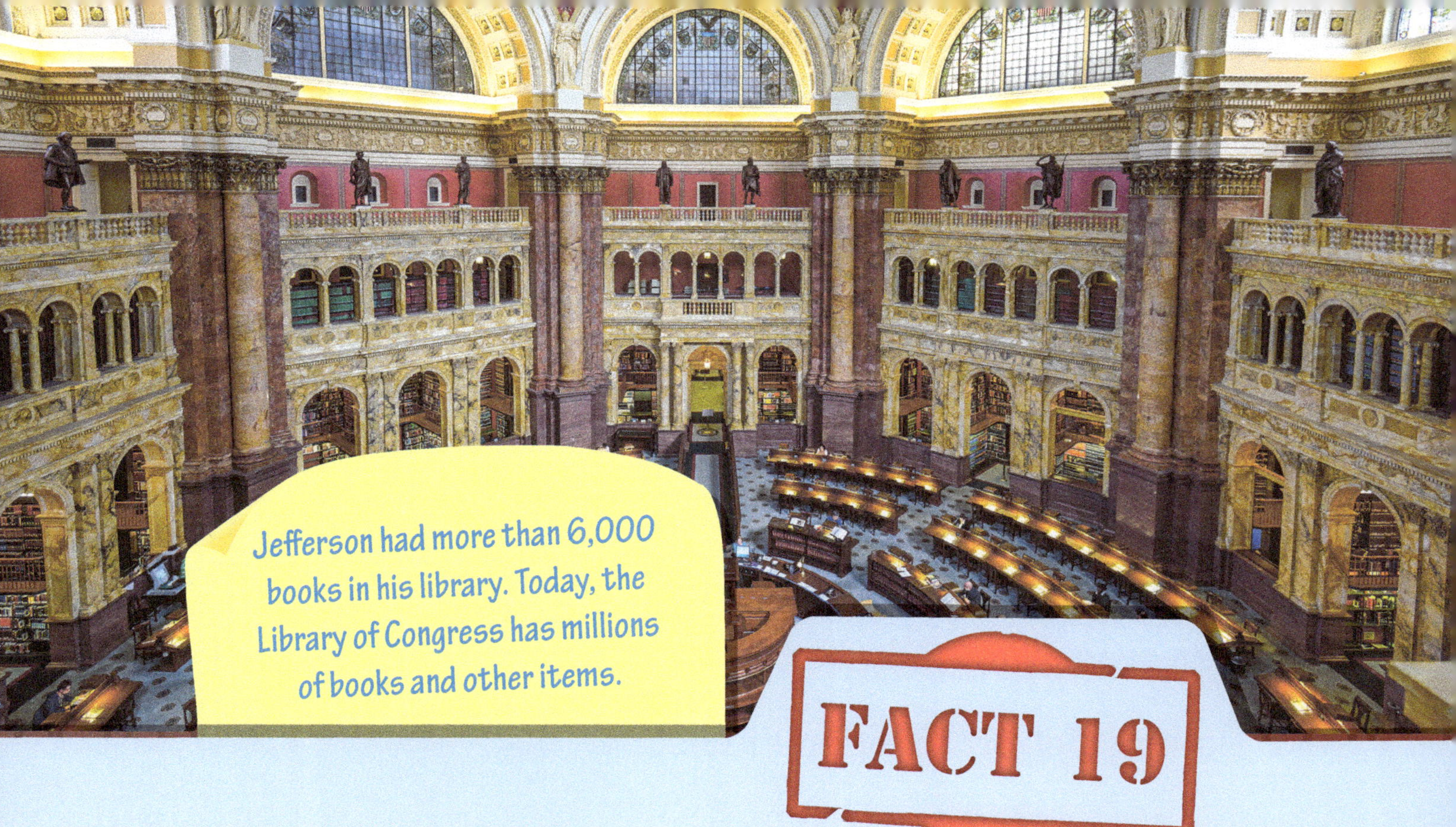

Jefferson had more than 6,000 books in his library. Today, the Library of Congress has millions of books and other items.

FACT 19

Jefferson sold his books to restart the Library of Congress.

Jefferson loved books and had one of the biggest personal libraries in the United States. During the War of 1812, British troops attacked the first Library of Congress in Washington, DC, and burned it down. Jefferson offered his books to restart the library.

FACT 20

Thomas Jefferson died on the Fourth of July.

Jefferson lived to be 83 years old. He died July 4, 1826, on the 50th anniversary of the signing of the Declaration of Independence, which is remembered as his greatest work. John Adams, another Founding Father and former president, died the same day.

Jefferson died at Monticello. He is buried on the grounds there.

Timeline

April 13, 1743 Thomas Jefferson is born in Virginia.

1757 Jefferson's father, Peter Jefferson, dies.

1768 Jefferson starts work on Monticello.

1769 Jefferson is elected to the House of Burgesses in Virginia.

1772 Jefferson marries Martha Wayles Skelton.

1775 Jefferson is named to the Second Continental Congress. The American Revolution begins.

1776 Jefferson writes the Declaration of Independence. The congress adopts it July 4.

1779 Jefferson is elected governor of Virginia.

1784 Jefferson goes to France. He lives there for 5 years.

1790 Jefferson becomes the first secretary of state.

1796 Jefferson runs for president, but doesn't win. He becomes vice president.

1800 Jefferson is elected president of the United States for the first time.

1803 Jefferson approves the Louisiana Purchase.

1804 Jefferson is elected president for a second time.

July 4, 1826 Jefferson dies on the 50th anniversary of the Declaration of Independence.

Jefferson Remembered

Today, we honor Thomas Jefferson as one of the United States' Founding Fathers. Jefferson's words in the Declaration of Independence still say a lot about this country and what it can be.

But even though we remember him as a leader of the country, Jefferson was a regular man, too. He liked to read and garden. He was interested in ancient creatures such as mastodons and enjoyed eating macaroni. What other fun facts can you find out about Thomas Jefferson?

The Jefferson Memorial stands in Washington, DC. It was dedicated on April 13, 1943, the 200th anniversary of Jefferson's birth.

Glossary

agriculture: the science of producing crops

architect: a person who designs, or plans, buildings

correspond: to send letters back and forth

delegate: a representative of one of the 13 colonies

draft: a piece of writing before it's finished

gadget: a tool, often small and sometimes unusual

inherit: to get by legal right after a person's death

minister: the representative of a country sent to another country

museum: a building in which things of interest are displayed

represent: to stand for

skeleton: the bony frame of the body

utter: to speak

For More Information

Books

Harris, Michael C. *What Is the Declaration of Independence?* New York, NY: Grosset & Dunlap, 2016.

Kalman, Maira. *Thomas Jefferson: Life, Liberty, and the Pursuit of Everything*. New York, NY: Nancy Paulsen Books, 2014.

Websites

The Monticello Classroom
classroom.monticello.org/kids/home/
Read about Thomas Jefferson, look at pictures of Monticello and its people, and even create your own house just like Jefferson did!

President Thomas Jefferson
ducksters.com/biography/uspresidents/thomasjefferson.php
Learn more facts about Jefferson and his presidency.

Publisher's note to educators and parents: Our editors have carefully reviewed these websites to ensure that they are suitable for students. Many websites change frequently, however, and we cannot guarantee that a site's future contents will continue to meet our high standards of quality and educational value. Be advised that students should be closely supervised whenever they access the Internet.

Index